My First Montessori Book of Colors

MARY DA PRATO

Copyright © 2013 Mary Da Prato

All rights reserved.

ISBN: 1484841875
ISBN-13: 978-1484841877

red

yellow

blue

orange

green

purple

brown

pink

gray

black

white

gradations of red

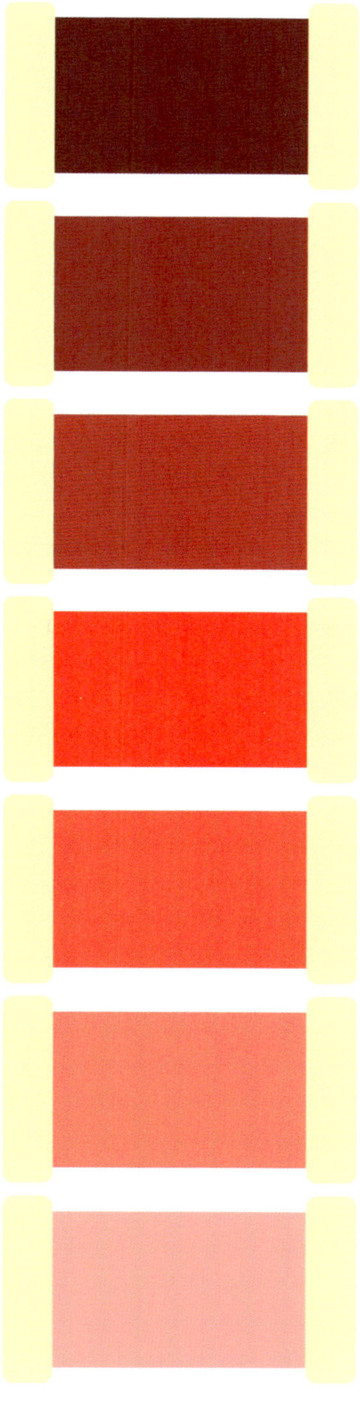

gradations of yellow

gradations of blue

gradations of orange

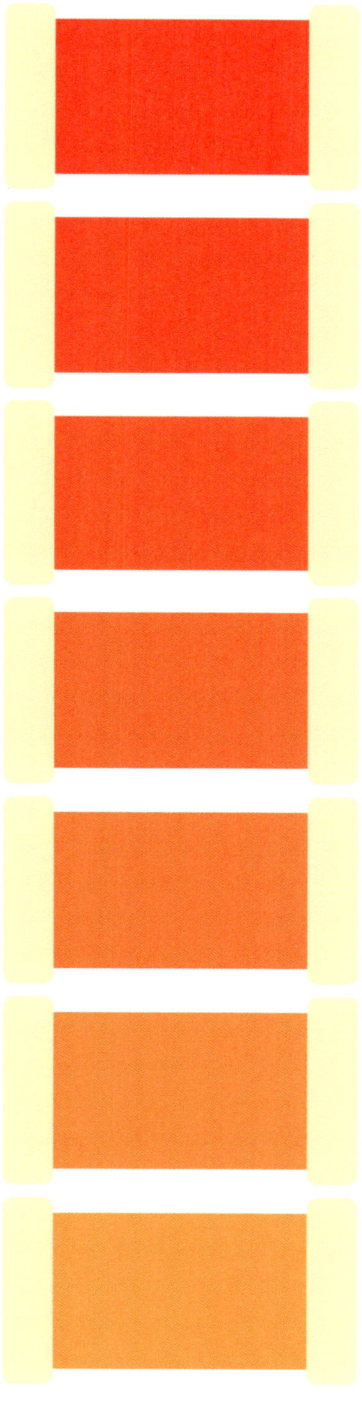

gradations of green

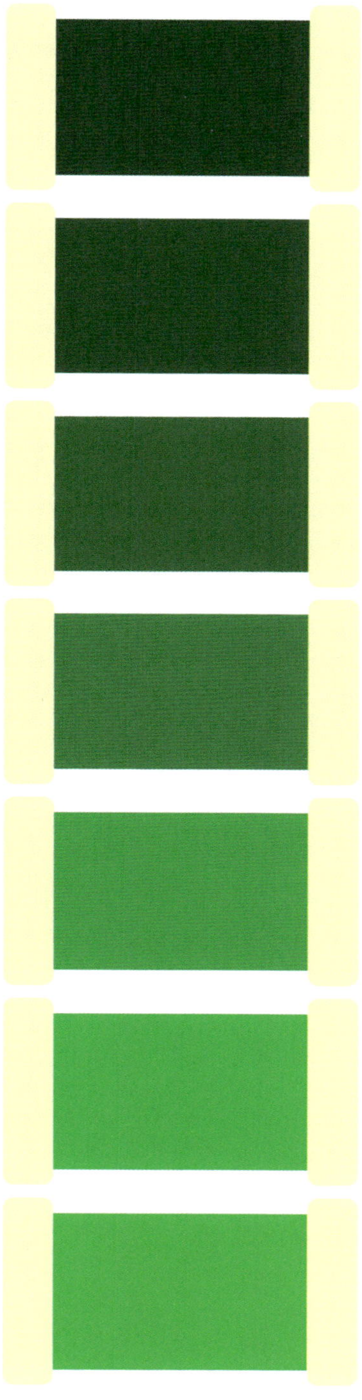

gradations of purple

gradations of brown

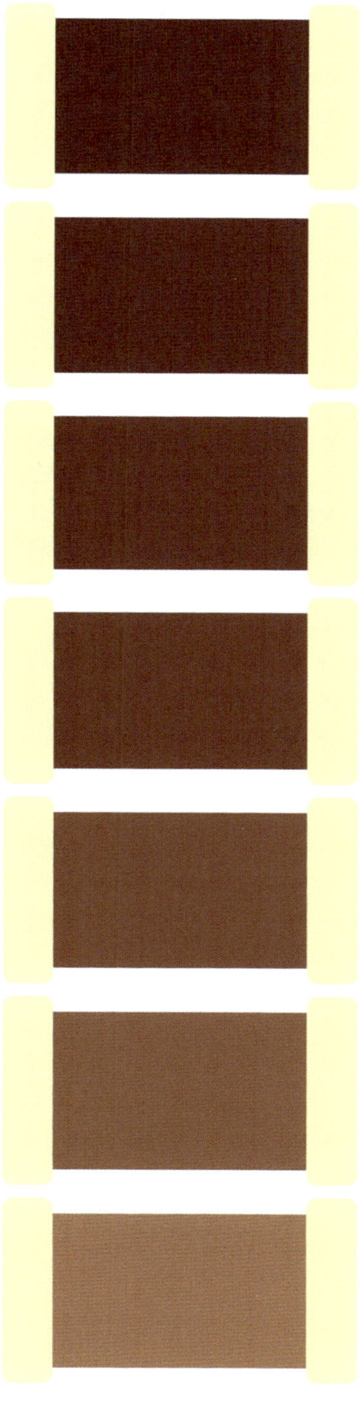

gradations of pink

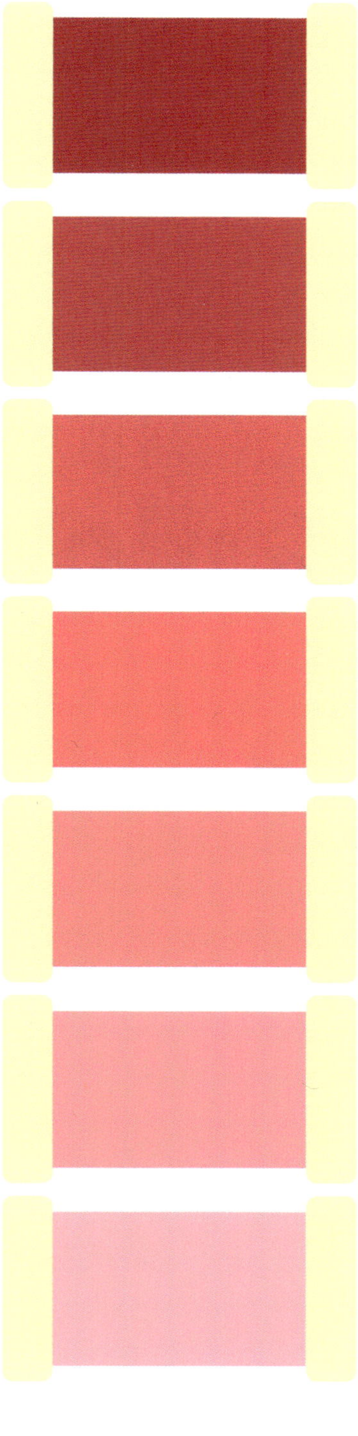

gradations of gray

FOR PARENTS

Diagrams in *My First Montessori Book of Colors* are inspired by hands-on Sensorial Color Tablet exercises in the Primary Montessori prepared environment. Pairing, or matching, Color Tablets is an activity initially introduced to children three years of age in the Montessori Casa. In Montessori, experience precedes language; therefore, color names are introduced following hands-on experience. Three-and-a-half to four year old children grade, or arrange, Color Tablets from light to dark and dark to light. Comparative language (i.e. lighter or darker) and superlative language (i.e. lightest or darkest) are introduced following successful grading. Children also compare Color Tablets to objects in their environment. Color Tablet lessons serve the following purposes:

- The sampling of Color Tablets provided in three Color Tablet boxes gives children keys to the world of color.
- Development of the chromatic sense and the ability to discriminate between colors, tints, and shades are refined.
- Gradations within the same color exist.
- Refinement of the visual perception of color develops a child's sense of aesthetics in preparation for art.
- Each color has a name.
- Work with Color Tablets aids imagination as children independently arrange tablets in different patterns, possibly discovering their arrangements make a color wheel.

In the Montessori Casa for three to six year old children, young students first explore color by matching primary colors red, blue, and yellow Color Tablets in pairs. Following success, additional Color Tablets such as secondary colors orange, green, and purple, are introduced. New color names are introduced three at a time once a child can successfully match them. When the child can pair all Color Tablets, the teacher invites the student to match tablets in the set to objects in the environment. For this exercise, the child pairs all tablets on the table and chooses one pair to match to the environment at a time. A button or stone is placed beside one of the tablets as a memory marker while the child locates and retrieves an object in the classroom that most closely matches the color without taking the tablet with him or her. This physical action helps the child retain what was learned, developing a better memory of color.

Gradation of Color Tablets from light to dark or dark to light is introduced following success with pairing and other grading activities in the classroom. Children begin by choosing one color to grade, such as blue. Later, the child may choose two or three sets of tablets to sort and grade simultaneously. Eventually, the child will be able to sort and grade all nine sets of tablets, a total of sixty-three.

You can explore the wonder of the chromatic sense with your child at home. Historically, Color Tablets have been made of a variety of materials including painted wood, spools of thread, embroidery thread wound on cards, or tile samples. Use materials that are available to you and your child. Alternatively, you can visit a paint store and ask the owner if any discontinued complimentary paint chips are available for your child to manipulate at home. Regardless of the materials you choose, observe the proper handling technique. Color Tablets should be handled by the edges to avoid soiling the color's surface with fingerprints which alter the color and change perception of the color.

Always supervise your child when using small objects as they are a choking hazard. Store them in a safe place following use and keep them away from younger siblings.

Other Titles in the *My First Montessori Book* Series

My First Montessori Book of Quantities

My First Montessori Book of Numbers

My First Montessori Book of Fractions

My First Montessori Book of Shapes

My First Montessori Book of Leaf Shapes

My First Montessori Book of Music Notation

My First Montessori Book of Land and Water Forms

Printed in Great Britain
by Amazon.co.uk, Ltd.,
Marston Gate.